1. Prologue

THERE is perhaps nothing extraordinary in the fact that man is wise and just, takes great care to provide for his own children, -shows due consideration for his parents, seeks sustenance for himself, protects himself against plots, and possesses all the other gifts of nature which are his. For man has been endowed with speech, of all things the most precious, and has been granted reason, which is of the greatest help and use.

Moreover, he knows how to reverence and worship the gods. But that dumb animals should by nature possess some good quality and should have many of man's amazing excellences assigned to them along with man, is indeed a remarkable fact. And to know accurately the special characteristics of each, and how living creatures also have been a source of interest no less than man, demands a trained intelligence and much learning. Now I am well aware of the labour that others have expended on this subject, yet I have collected all the materials that I could; I have clothed them in untechnical language, and am persuaded that my achievement is a treasure far from negligible. So if anyone considers them profitable, let him make use of them; anyone who does not consider them so may give them to his father to keep and attend to.

For not all things give pleasure to all men, nor do all men consider all subjects worthy of study. Although I was born later than many accomplished writers of an earlier day, the accident of date ought not to mulct me of praise, if I too produce a learned work whose ampler research and whose choice of language make it deserving of serious attention.

2. Sacred Fish at Myra

There is a bay at Myra in Lycia and it has a spring and there is a shrine of Apollo there, and the priest of this god scatters the flesh of calves that have been sacrificed to the god, and Sea-perch come swimming up in shoals and eat the flesh, as though they were guests invited to the feast.
And the sacrificers are delighted, for they believe that this feasting of the fishes is a good omen for them, and they say that the god is propitious because the fish gorged themselves upon the flesh. If however the fish cast the food ashore with their tails as though they despised it and regarded it as tainted, this is believed to signify the wrath of the god.
And the fish recognise the priest's voice, and if they obey his summons they gladden those on whose behalf they have been summoned; in the opposite event they cause them grief.

Sacred Fish at Hierapolis

Animal Peculiarity Volume 3 Part 4

By T.P Just

~~~

Get All The Books In The Series:

Animal Peculiarity Volume 1 {1-8]
Animal Peculiarity Volume 2 {1-8]
Animal Peculiarity Volume3 {1-8]
Just Enterprises

Table of Contents

In the ancient Bambyce (it is now called Hierapolis since Seleucus gave it this name) there are sacred fish which swim in companies and have leaders; these are the first to eat of the food which is thrown in to them. More than all other fish do they maintain friendly relations with one another and are always at peace, either because the goddess " inspires them with unanimity, or because being satisfied with the food that is thrown in to them, they therefore abstain from eating one another and know nothing of it.

3. A Monstrous Lamb

The Egyptians assert (though they are far from convincing me), they assert, I say, that in the days of the far—famed Bocchoris a Lamb was born with eight feet and two tails, and that it spoke.

They say also that this Lamb had two heads and four horns. It is right to forgive Homer who bestows speech upon Xanthus the horse. for Homer is a poet And Alcman could not be censured for imitating Homer in such matters, for the first venture of Homer is a plea sufficient to justify forgiveness. But how can one pay any regard to Egyptians who exaggerate like this? However fabulous though they be, I have related the peculiarities of this lamb.

4. The Hawk: various species

Here is another fact touching Hawks that I remember to have heard. Before the Nile inundates Egypt and comes up over the ploughlands Hawks shed their old feathers just as the branches of trees shed their withered leaves, and grow new and beautiful plumage as trees do foliage.

It seems that there are in fact several species of Hawks, and Aristophanes appears to hint as much. But we have dispatched three thousand Hawks, mounted archers. And each one moves forward with talons crooked-—kestrel, buzzard, vulture, night-hawk, eagle.

They are allotted separately to many gods. The partridge-catcher, they say, and the ocypterus are servants of Apollo; the lammergeier and the shearwater they assign to Athena; the dove-killer is said to be the darling of Hermes, the wide—wing, of Hera, and the buzzard, as it is called, of Artemis.

To the Mother of the Gods (they assign) the mermnus, and to one god one bird, to another. There are in fact a great many kinds of Hawks.

5. The Marten and Alcmena

The Egyptians incur the derision at any rate of most people for worshiping and deifying various kinds of animals. But the inhabitants of Thebes, although Greeks, worship a marten, so I hear, and allege that it was the nurse of Heracles, or if it was not the nurse, yet when Alcmena was in labour and unable to bring her child to birth, the marten ran by her and loosed the bonds of her womb, so that Heracles delivered and at once began to crawl. And those who live in Hamaxitus in the Troad worship: a Mouse, and that is why.

The Mouse worshipped in the Troad

According to them, they give the name of Sminthian to Apollo whom they worship, for the Aeolians and the people of the Troad still call a mouse sminthus, just as Aeschylus too in his Sisyphus, writes

'Nay, but what smintheus of the fields is so monstrous? '

And in the temple of Smintheus tame Mice are kept and fed at the public expense, and beneath the altar white Mice have their nests, and by the tripod of Apollo there stands a Mouse. And I have also heard the following mythical tale about this cult. Mice came in tens of thousands and cut off before they ripened the crops of the Aeolians and Trojans, rendering the harvest barren for the sowers.

Accordingly the god at Delphi said when they enquired of him, that they must sacrifice to Apollo Smintheus; they obeyed and freed themselves from the conspiracy of Mice, and their wheat attained the normal harvest.

And they add the following story. Some Cretans who owing to a disaster that befell them were sent out to found a colony, besought the Pythian Apollo to tell them of some good place where it would be advantageous to found a city.

There issued from the oracle this answer: in the place where the earth-born made war upon them, there they should settle and raise a city. So they came to this place Hamaxitus and pitched their camp in order to rest; but a countless swarm of Mice crept stealthily upon them, gnawed through their shield — straps and ate through their bow- strings.

So they guessed that these were the 'earth-born ' referred to, and, besides, having now no means of getting weapons of defence, they settled in this spot and built a temple to Apollo Smintheus, Well, this mention of Mice has led us to touch upon a matter of theology; however we are none the worse for having listened even to such tales as this,

6. The Dolphins and its dead

It seems that Dolphins are mindful even of their dead and by no means abandon their fellows when they have departed this life. At any rate they get underneath their dead companion and then carry him along to the shore, confident that men will bury him and Aristotle bears witness to this.

And another company of Dolphins follow them by way of doing honour to, or even actually fighting to protect, the dead body, for fear lest some other great fish should rush up, seize it, and. then devour it. All just men who appreciate music bury dead Dolphins out of respect for their love of music. But those to whom, as they say, the Muses and the Graces are alien care nothing for Dolphins. And so, beloved Dolphins, you must pardon the savage nature of man, since even the people of Athens cast out the excellent Phocion at unburied. And even Olympians lay unburied, although she was the mother of the son of Zeus, as she herself boasted and as he asserted.

And the, Egyptians after killing the Roman Pompey, surnamed 'the Great,' who had achieved so much, who had had such distinguished victories and had celebrated three triumphs, had saved the life of his murderer's father and had re-established him on the throne of Egypt, left him cast out, a headless corpse, by the sea, just as men often leave you. For this all-devouring creature man does not even spare you, but goes so far as to pickle you, and is unconscious that his action is hateful to the Muses, the daughters of Zeus.

7. The Lion of Egypt

In Egypt they worship Lions, and there is a city called after them. It is worth recording the peculiarities of the Lions there. They have temples and very many spaces in which to roam; the flesh of oxen is supplied to them daily and it lies, stripped of bones and sinews, scattered here and there, and the Lions eat to the accompaniment of song in the Egyptian language. And the theme of the song is 'Do not bewitch any of the beholders'; this singing appears, as you might say, to be a substitute for amulets. Many of the Lions are deified in Egypt, and there are chambers face to face consecrated to their use. The windows of some open to the east, others to the west, making life more pleasant for them. And to preserve their health they have places for exercise, and wrestling—grounds nearby, and their adversary is a well—nourished calf. And if, after practicing his skill against the calf, the Lion brings it down (this takes time for he is lazy and unused to hunting), he eats his fill and goes back to his own stall.

The Lion is a very fiery animal and this is why the Egyptians connect him with Hephaestus, but, they say, he dislikes and shuns the fire from without because of the great fire within himself. And since he is of a very fiery nature, they say the Lion is the house of the Sun, and when the sun is at its hottest and the height of summer, they say it is approaching the Lion. Moreover the inhabitants of the great city of Heliopolis keep these Lions in the entrance to the temples of the god as sharing (so the Egyptians say) to some extent the lot of the gods. And further, they appear in dreams to those whom the god regards with favour and utter prophecies, and those who have committed perjury they punish not after some delay but immediately, for the god inspire them with a righteous indignation.

And Empedocles maintains that if his lot translates a man into an animal, then it is best for him to transmigrate into a lion; if into a plant, then into a sweet bay. Empedocles words are 'Among beasts they become lions that couch upon the mountains and sleep on the earth, and among trees with fair foliage sweet-bay-trees.'

The Sphinx

But we are (as we ought) to take into consideration the Wisdom of the Egyptians who refer such manifestations to natural causes, they assign the fore- parts of this animal to fire, and the hinder parts to fusing the body of a maiden with that of a lion. And Euripides suggests this when he says   'And drawing her tail in beneath her lion's feet she sat down."

The Nemean Lion

And moreover they say that the Lion of Nemea fell from the moon. At any rate Epimenides also has these words:
' For I am sprung from the fair-tressed Moon, who in a fearful shudder shook off the savage lion in Nemea, and brought him forth at the bidding of Queen Hera.'

Let us however relegate these matters to the region of myth; but the peculiarities of Lions have been sufficiently dealt with both earlier on and in the present chapter.

8. The Wax-moth

The Wax-moth is a creature that delights in the brilliance of fire and flies to lamps burning brightly, but falls into them owing to its momentum and is burned to death. And Aeschylus the Tragic poet mentions it in these words ' I greatly dread the foolish fate of the wax- moth.'

9. The Wagtail

The Wagtail is a winged creature weak in its hinder parts, and that is why (they say) it is in- capable of building a nest of its own accord or for itself, but lays its eggs in the nests of other birds. Hence in the proverbs of country folk poor men are called 'wag tails'. The bird moves its tail-feathers, like the Ceryl in the passage of Archilochus. And Aristophanes also mentions this bird in his Amphiaraus thus: '
 Give the old man's loins a thorough shaking, as the Wagtail does, and work a powerful spell.'
And in his Geras 'Rhythmic wagtail — gait of a belly-arching fellow.'
And Autocrates in his Tympanistae:
As sweet maidens, daughters of Lydia, sport and lightly leap and clap their hands in the temple of Artemis the Fair at Ephesus, now sinking down upon their haunches and again springing up, like the hopping wagtail.'

Two proverbs :(a) the Mouse

When Mice die a natural death and not through any design upon them, their limbs dissolve and little by little they depart this life. That, you see, is the origin of the saying ' Like a mouse's death,' and Menander mentions it in his Thais

(b)The Turtle Dove

And men commonly say ' More talkative than a turtle-dove,' because the turtle-dove not only never stops uttering through its mouth, but they do say that it utters a great deal through its hinder parts also. And the same writer mentions this proverb in his Necklace. And Demetrhis play Sicelia mentions that turtle—doves chatter through their rump as well.

The Mouse, its character

They say that Mice are exceedingly salacious, and they cite Cratinus as a witness, when he says in his Drapetides (Runaway slave—girls):
Look you; from a clear sky will I blast with lightning the debauchery of that mouse Xenophon,'
And they say that the female mouse is even more madly amorous. And again from the Chorus of Epicrates they cite these words:
The accursed go-between fooled me completely, swearing by the Maiden, by Artemis, by Persephone, that the wench was a heifer, a virgin, an untamed filly—and all the time she was an absolute mouse hole.'
By calling her an' absolute mouse hole ' he meant to say that she was beyond measure lecherous. And Philemon says:
A white mouse, when someone tries to-but I am ashamed to say the word, the confounded woman at once lets out such a yell, that it is often impossible to avoid attracting attention.'

10. Onuphis, the sacred bull

The Egyptians also worship a black bull which they call Onuphis. And the name of the place where it is reared let the Egyptian narratives tell us, for it is a hard name. Its hair grows the opposite way to that on other bulls; that is another of its peculiarities. The go-between is humorously depicted as not knowing that 'the Maiden' and 'Persephone' is one and the same person.

Peculiarities, It is larger, it seems; than; all other bulls, even than those of Chaonia which the inhabitants of Thesprotia and Epirus call 'fatted,' tracing their descent from the oxen of Geryones. This Onuphis is fed upon Lucerne.

The Dolphin

It seems that the Dolphin is swifter and can leap higher than all other fish, in fact than all land animals also. At any rate it leaps even over a vessel as Aristotle says ; and he attempts to assign a cause for this, which is as follows.

It holds its breath as divers do when under water. For, you know, divers straining the breath in their bodies, let it go like a bowstring, and with it their bodies like an arrow ; and, says Aristotle, the breath compressed inside them thrusts and shoots them upwards.

The 'Physa' fish

The Physa is an Egyptian fish that fills one with astonishment, for it knows, they say, when the Moon is waning and when it is waxing. Moreover its liver grows or dwindles as that goddess does: at one time it is well nourished, at another it is more shrunken.

11. The Catfish

The Catfish is found in the Maeander and the Lycus, the rivers of Asia Minor, and in the Strymon in Europe, and resembles the European sheath-fish. It is of all fishes the most devoted to its offspring.

At any rate the female after parturition ceases to pay attention to her children, newly given birth, whereas the male takes charge of the young things, stays by them, and wards off every attempt upon them. And he is quite capable, according to Aristotle, of swallowing a fish—hook.

Frog and Water-snake

The Frog abhors and greatly dreads the water. Accordingly, in return it tries to terrify and scare the water-snake by its loud croaking.

The Crocodile

The malice of the Crocodile in its pursuit of men and other animals (is shown by the following example) When it knows the path by which men come down to a river either to draw water or to water a horse or a camel or even to embark on a vessel, it floods the track with a quantity of water by night and filling its mouth, pours the contents on the path again and again, meaning to make it slippery and to render the capture easier for itself.

For when (men or animals) slip they do not retain their hold on the gang-plank but fall off, whereupon the Crocodile, leaping up, seizes and makes a meal of them. I have still to mention a few facts touching Crocodiles. This animal is not well-disposed to every species of Egyptian plover (and there are many species, with names harsh and repulsive to the ear, and so I omit them).

12. The Clapperbill

This animal is I not well-disposed to every species of Egyptian plover (and there are many species, with names harsh and repulsive to the ear, and so I omit them) ; it is only the Clapperbill,b as it is called, that and the it treats as companion and friend, for this bird is Clapperbill able to pick off the leeches without coming to harm.

13. Democritus on the fecundity of certain animals

Democritus states that the Pig and the Dog Democritus bring forth many at a birth, and he assigns the cause to the fact that they have many wombs and many certain animals places for the reception of semen.

Now the seed does not fill them all at a single ejaculation, but these animals Copulate twice or three times in order that the continuance of the act may fill the receptacles of the seed. Mules however, he says, do not give birth, for they have not got wombs like other animals but of a different formation and quite incapable of receiving seed; for the mule is not the product of nature but a surreptitious contrivance of the ingenuity and, so to say, adulterous daring of man.

14. The Libyan Ass and Mares

And I fancy, said Democritus, that a mare became pregnant from being by chance violated by any ass, and that men were its pupils in this deed of violence, and presently accustomed themselves to the use of the offspring.

And it is especially the asses of Libya which, being very big, mounts mares that have no manes, having been clipped. For those who know about the coupling of horses say that a mare in possession of the glory of her mane would never tolerate such a mate.

15. Democritus on the effects of climate on the animal foetus

Democritus says that the foetus is dropped more easily in southern countries than in northern; and this is natural because the south wind makes the bodies of pregnant females relax and expand. So as the shelter has been loosened and is no longer closefitting , the embryo grows warm and the heat causes it to slip this way and that and to drop out with greater ease.

If however there is a frost and the north wind is blowing, the embryo is congealed and is not easily moved, and is not rocked as it were by a wave, but as though it were in a wave less calm, remains firm and taut and endures until the time ordained by nature for its birth.

And so in cold, according to the philosopher of Abdera, the foetus remains in its place, but in warmth it is generally ejected. For when the heat is excessive, he says that the veins and sex-organs are bound to expand.

Democritus and the horns of Deers

And the same writer says that the reason why Deer grow horns is as follows. He agrees that their stomach is extremely hot, and that the veins through- out their entire body are extremely fine, while the bone containing the brain is extremely thin, like a membrane, and loose in texture, and the veins that rise from it to the crown of the head are extremely thick.

The food at all events, or at any rate the most productive part of it, is distributed through the body at great speed: the fatty portion of it, he says, envelops their body on the outside, while the solid portion mounts through the veins to the brain, And this is how horns, being moistened with plentiful juices, come to sprout.

The continuous flow therefore extrudes the earlier horns. And the moisture which rises and emerges from the body solidifies the air concealing and hardening it into horns, while that which is still enclosed in the body is soft. The one portion is rendered solid by the external cold; the other remains soft owing to the internal heat.

Accordingly the added growth of the new horn extrudes the old was alien, because. What is within chafes and, tries to push it upwards, swelling and throbbing as though it were in haste to be born and to emerge, for the juice, you see, bursting out and mounting upwards from below cannot remain stationary, but it too solidifies and is impelled against the parts above it.

And the older horns are in most cases forced out by the strength of that which is within, although in some cases the animal, forced ahead by its own momentum, has broken of horns that have got entangled in branches and hinder it from running swiftly. These then drop off, but the new horns which are ready to peep out are pushed forward by nature.

Democritus on the growth of horns in Oxen

Castrated oxen, says Democritus, grow curved, thin, and long horns; whereas those of un- castrated Oxen are thick at the base, straight, and of shorter length. And he says that these have a much wider forehead than the others, for as there are many veins in that part, the bones are in con- sequence broader.

And the growth of the horns being thicker makes that part of the animal broader, whereas castrated Oxen in which the circumference at the base of the horns is but small, have a narrower forehead, says he.

Democritus on hornless Bulls

But hornless Bulls, not possessing the 'honey- combed' part of the forehead (so Democritus styles it; his meaning would be 'porous') , since the entire bone is solid and does not permit the conflux of the body's juices are unprotected and destitute of the means of self-defense.

And since the veins in this bone are somewhat under-nourished, they grow thinner and feebler. The neck too is of necessity drier in hornless Bulls, for the veins in it also are thinner. And that is why the veins are not so strong. But all the Arabian cows that have finely developed horns, have them (he says) because the copious influx of animal juices promotes the splendid growth of the horns.

But even Arabian cows are hornless when they have the frontal bone that receives the Moist secretions too solid and unreceptive of the animal juices. In a word, this influx is the cause of growth in horns, and the flow is introduced where the veins are most numerous, thickest, and as full of moisture as they can hold.

16. Eagle saves the baby Gilgamos

A love of man is another characteristic of Eagle saves the baby animals. At any rate an Eagle fostered a baby. And I want to tell the whole story so that I may have evidence of my proposition. When Seuechorus was king of Babylon the Chaldeans foretold that the-son, born of his daughter would wrest the kingdom from his grandfather.

This made him afraid and (if I may be allowed, the small jest) he played Acrisius to his daughter he put the strictest of watches upon her. For all that, since fate was cleverer than the king of Babylon, the girl became a mother, being pregnant by some obscure man. So the guards from fear of the King hurled the infant from the citadel, for that was where the aforesaid girl was imprisoned.

Now an Eagle which saw with its piercing eye the child while still falling, before it was dashed to the earth, flew beneath it, flung its back under it, and conveyed it to some garden and set it down with the utmost care. But when the keeper of the place saw the pretty baby he fell in love with it and nursed it ; and it was called Gilgamos and became king of Babylon.

If anyone regards this as a legend, I, after testing it to the best of my ability, concur in the verdict. I have heard however that Achaemenes the Persian; from whom the Persian aristocracy are descended, was nursed by an Eagle.

Dogs at Rhocca
In Crete there is a temple to Artemis Dogs at Rhoccaea, as she is called. The dogs there go raving mad. So when they are afflicted, with this disease they hurl themselves lead foremost from the promontory into the sea.

Tame Lions in Elam
In the country of Elam there is a shrine to Tame Lions Anaitis and there are tame lions there which welcome and fawn upon those on their way to the shrine. And if you call them while you are eating they come like guests invited to a meal, and after taking whatever you offer they depart in a modest and becoming manner.

The Water Phoenix
In the Red Sea, so, they say, there is a fish, and its name is the 'Water-Phoenix'. It has black stripes, and between them it is speckled with dark blue dots.

17. The Horse mackerel

The Horse-mackerel in the Red Sea is the same length as that which occurs in our sea: its body is encircled with stripes like gold which extend from the gills to the tail, and a silvery stripe parts them in two. Its mouth is open and the lower jaw projects beyond the upper; its eyes are green and are surrounded by lids of a golden colour.

18. The Charax

The fish called Charax is another product of the same sea. It has fins, and the lateral ones are like gold in appearance, and so are all its dorsal fins. On the lower part of its body are rings of purple, but the tail, believe me, is golden, while purple dots colour beautifully the centre of its eyes.

The Archer fish

The Archer, which occurs in the same sea, resembles the sea-urchin in appearance and has, Ash hard, long prickles.

The Porcupine

The Porcupines of Libya administer a sharp prick to those who touch them and even cause severe pains. Even when dead their bristles can give a nasty stab, so they say.

19. The Red Sea 'Monkey'

There is also a Monkey in the Red Sea; it is not a fish but a cartilaginous creature, and not large at that. And this sea-monkey resembles the, land-monkey in colour, and its face is ape-like. But the rest of its body is protected by a sheath, not like a fish but resembling that of a tortoise.

It is also somewhat flat-nosed, as the land-monkey is. But the rest of its body is a flat shape like the torpedo, so that one might say that it was a bird without, spread wings ; at any rate when swimming it looks like a bird in flight.

But it differs from the land-monkey in this way: it is speckled, and the flat parts on the nape of the neck are red, and so are the gills. It has a large mouth at the extremity of its face, and in this respect also the fish bears a natural resemblance to the shape of the land-monkey.

Change of colour in birds and fishes

During the summer the Nightingale assumes, change of a different colour and alters its note, for its song is not resonant and varied but different from its song fishes in spring.

The blackbird sings in summertime, but in winter it utters a chattering and confused sound, and changing its colour like a garment, from being black appears light brown. And the thrush in winter appears somewhat speckled, whereas in summer it displays a mottled neck.

The following fish too change their colour, various wrasses (ciclae, cossyphi; and phycides), and sprats. And jackals, according, to Aristotle, are hairless throughout, and the summer but in winter have thick coats.

20. The Nile Perch

At Bubastus in Egypt there is a pool and it fosters an immense multitude of Nile Perch, and these are tame and the gentlest of fish. People throw in morsels of bread to them, and they leap up, each trying to jump quicker than the other, and pick out the food that is being thrown in.

This fish is also found in rivers, for instance in the Cydnus in Cilicia; but there it is small. And the reason is that a stream which is clear, pure, and cold besides (for such is the Cydnus) does not afford it plentiful nourishment, for the fish prefers turbid water full of mud, and fattens on it.

But the Pyramus and the Sarus breed larger kinds; these also are rivers of Cilicia. And" it must be the same fish that are bred in the Syrian Orontes, but the largest of all are bred in the river Ptolemaeus and in the lake of Apamea.

21. Tame fish of various lands

Tame fishes which answer to a call and gladly accept food are to be found, and are kept in many places, in Epirus for instance, at the town formerly called Stephancpolis, in the temple of Fortune the cisterns on either side of the ascent; at Helorus ltoopin Sicily which was once a Syracusai fortress; and at the shrine of Zeus of Labranda in a spring of transparent water.

And there fish have golden necklaces and earrings also of gold. The shrine of this Zeus is 70 stades distant from the city of Mylasa; A' sword is-, attached to the side of the statue, and the god is worshipped under the name of 'Zeus of Caria ' and 'God of War,' for the Carians were the first to think, of making a trade of war and to serve as soldiers for pay, to fit arm-straps to their shields, and to fix plumes on their helmets. And they were called 'Carians' after Car the son of Creta and Zeus, and Zeus received the title of Labrahdeus because he sent down furious (labros) and heavy rainstorms. And in Chiosi in what is called 'The Old Men's Harbour' there are multitudes of tame fish, which the inhabitants of Chios keep to solace the declining years of "the very aged.

And in the country that lies between the Euphrates and the Tigris there is a spring which is celebrated; as being transparent to; the bottom and as sending forth bright, clear water, which as it brims over becomes the river.

Aborras. And the people of the country attach a sacred story to the name; which is as, follows. After her marriage with Zeus Hera bathed 'herself there, so the Syrians say, and to this day-the spot exhales a fragrance; and all the round about is permeated with it; And there tame fishes garnbol in shoals.

22. The sons of Aristodemus and the Delphic oracle

Even the gods do not disdain to take cognizance of the characteristics of animals. At any rate I learn that Eurysthenes and Procleus, the sons of Aristodemus, son of Aristomachus, son of Cleodas, son of Hyllus the son of Heracles, wishing to Wed, went to Delphi to ask the god with whom, whether Greek or barbarian, they should ally themselves in order to appear as having made a prosperous and wise marriage. And the god answered: Go back to Sparta, returning by the Way you came, and wherever the fiercest animal carrying the gentlest meets you, their plight your troth; for that will be better for you.

So they obeyed and arrived in the territory of Cleonae. where a wolf met them carrying a lamb which it had snatched from a flock. So they reckoned that the oracle meant these animals, and they took the daughters of Thersander, son of Cleonymus, a man of good repute to wife. Now if the gods know what animal is, the gentlest and what the fiercest, it is not unfitting that we too should know their natures.

The land of India bears a great number and The Snakes variety of creatures. And some are evidence of, its beneficent and wonderful fertility, others are not to be envied nor such as one can commend or desire. Something about those that are profitable or are luxuries of great price I have already said; more; shall be; please god, said hereafter.

But for the present I intend to describe how the earth shows the pain with which it bears snakes. Many and various are the snakes it bears Now these snakes yare injurious to man and all other animals.

But the same land produces herbs that counteract their bites, and the natives have experience and knowledge of them, and have observed which drug is an antidote to which ,snake and come to one, another's aid with all possible speed in their effort to arrest the very violent and rapid spread of the poison throughout the body.

And the country produces these drugs in generous abundance to help when needed.' But any snake that kills a man, so, the Indians say(and they cite numerous witnesses from Libya and the inhabitants of; Egyptian Thebes), can no longer descend and creep into its own home the earth declines to receive it, but casts it out like exile from its own bosom.

Thenceforward it moves around, a vagabond and wanderer, living in distress beneath the open sky throughout summer and winter; none of its mates goes near it any more, nor do those which it has begotten recognize their sire. Such is the punishment for manslaughter which nature has shown to befall even dumb animals [it is by divine providence], as my memory tells me. This is said for the instruction of persons of understanding.

23. The Geese of the Capitol

Dogs are less useful at keeping watch than geese, as the Romans discovered. At any rate the Celts were at war with them, and had thrust them back with overwhelming force and were in the city itself; indeed they had captured Rome, except for the hill of the Capitol, for that was not easy for them to scale.

For all the spots which seemed open to assault by stratagem had been prepared for defence. It was the time at which Marcus Manlius, the consul, was guarding the aforesaid height as entrusted to him.

(It was he, you remember, who garlanded his son for his gallant conduct, but put him to death for deserting his post.) But when the Celts observed that the place was inaccessible to them on every side, they decided to wait for the dead of night and then fall upon the Romans when fast asleep and they hoped to scale the rock where it was unguarded and unprotected, since the Romans were confident that the Gauls would not attack from that quarter.

And as a result Manlius himself and the Citadel of Jupiter would have been captured with the utmost ignominy, had not some geese chanced to• be there. For dogs fall silent when food is thrown to them, but it is a peculiarity of geese to cackle and make a din when things are thrown to them to eat.

And so with their cries they roused. Manlius and the guards sleeping around him. This is the reason why up to the present day dogs at Rome annually pay the penalty of death in memory of their ancient treachery, but on stated days a goose is honoured by being borne along on a litter in great state.

Get All The Books In The Series:

Animal Peculiarity Volume 1 {1-8]
Animal Peculiarity Volume 2 {1-8]
Animal Peculiarity Volume3 {1-8]

www.ingramcontent.com/pod-product-compliance
Lightning Source LLC
Chambersburg PA
CBHW050847290526
45792CB00002B/556